Patricia Smith's

Album of
ALL BISQUE
Dolls

IDENTIFICATION & VALUE GUIDE

COLLECTOR BOOKS
A Division of Schroeder Publishing Co., Inc.

The current values in this book should be used only as a guide. They are not intended to set prices, which vary from one section of the country to another. Auction prices as well as dealer prices vary greatly and are affected by condition as well as demand. Neither the Author nor the Publisher assumes responsiblity for any losses that might be incurred as a result of consulting this guide.

Searching For A Publisher?

We are always looking for knowledgeable people considered to be experts within their fields. If you feel that there is a real need for a book on your collectible subject and have a large comprehensive collection, contact us.

COLLECTOR BOOKS
P.O. Box 3009
Paducah, Kentucky 42002-3009

Additional copies of this book may be ordered from:

Collector Books
P.O. Box 3009
Paducah, KY 42002–3009

@ $14.95. Add $2.00 for postage and handling.

Copyright: Patricia Smith, 1992

This book or any part thereof may not be reproduced without the written consent of the Author and Publisher.

1 2 3 4 5 6 7 8 9 0

Printed by IMAGE GRAPHICS, INC., Paducah, Kentucky

Dedication

Thanks go to Shirley Bertrand who invited us to her home and allowed us to "trash" her personal collection and doll cases. Nothing seemed to fit back from where it came! Although the photography sessions were trying, and tiring, Shirley was a true lady – and a good cook. We were well fed. Shirley is a very loyal and understanding friend, a true "one of a kind" human being. The world could do with about 250 million more like her.

Credits

The majority of photographs are from the collection of Shirley Bertrand of Shirley's Doll House, P.O. Box 99A, Wheeling, IL 60090.

Many thanks to the following who also shared their dolls for the production of this book: Gloria Anderson, Stan Buler, Sandra Cummins, Ellen Dodge, Frasher Doll Auctions (Rt. 1, Box 142, Oak Grove, MO 64075), Patty Martin, Mary McArthur, Bonnie Stewart, Turn of Century Antiques (1475 Broadway, Denver, CO), Kathy Tvrdik, Jane Walker, and Glorya Woods.

Cover Photos

TOP RIGHT: 8½" "Coquette" made with one-piece body and head and wearing original dress. Has molded hair and ribbon, painted features and jointed at shoulders and hips. Head modeled tilted to side. Painted-on socks and Mary Jane-style shoes that tie in front. Made in Germany by Gebruder Heubach. $850.00.

BOTTOM LEFT: 5½" Dutch googly dolls. They are "nodders" which means the heads bob when touched. Jointed at neck only; rest of the body is made of one piece. Both made in Japan. Pair – $265.00.

BOTTOM RIGHT: 7" woman with both arms and hands modeled away from body. Her head is leaning on her shoulder. Her long-waisted top has applied blue rose. Attached to original pincushion base with sewn-on legs. Made in Germany. $485.00.

Table of Contents

Foreword

The subject of "All Bisque" covers a vast amount of dolls and figurines that find their way into most doll collections, antique or modern. Maybe the reason is that they are small and do not take up much cabinet space, and the price on most is still reasonable when compared with most areas of doll collecting.

What constitutes quality in these little dolls is the very same as the larger, more elaborate dolls – artist workmanship. If the quality of the bisque or china is excellent and the artwork is extremely well done, then the piece in your collection is above average. In all bisque items, both the excellent and the poor quality came from Germany and Japan. There are badly painted German dolls and detailed painted dolls from Japan. Each has to be gauged on its own merit.

In this value guide, artist workmanship determines price. Above average artistry constitutes an above average "book" price. The same holds for below average "book" prices – poor quality; lower price. (Or it should!) Prices are based on average dolls with good workmanship and no damage, such as chips, cracks, nicks, or breaks.

Most doll collectors will enjoy finding the little dolls in this album. Hopefully going through this album will make each collector desire "just one more."

French All Bisque Dolls

The little all bisque dolls made in France are the most desirable of the all bisque made dolls. True French-made dolls are hard to authenticate and very expensive due to rarity. The following are physical indications of a possible French-made doll.

They will have a swivel head (socket head) with the neck part lined with kid leather. Most will have the French loop molded onto the base of the head. These loops are easily identified as they look like the tops of a bell.

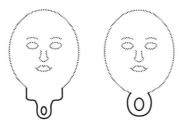

Many French-type all bisque dolls are peg jointed at the hips and shoulders. Some will have painted eyes, but the majority have glass eyes. They will have feather painted eyebrows and not painted with one stroke.

The French type have much thinner legs and are more delicate than the German-made dolls. They can be barefooted, but they can also have stockings (vertical ribbed or circular ribbed), coming to the knees or above. These dolls can have high top, pointed-toed boots, buttoned boots, or footwear with four or more painted ankle straps.

French-type dolls generally have excellent quality bisque that is artistically painted. Many have tiny cork pates in the open crowns of the head.

To command the following prices, the doll must be in overall excellent condition with no hairline cracks, or chips.

IDENTIFIED/ACCEPTED FRENCH WITH SWIVEL HEAD, GLASS EYES: Molded-on boots and hose. 4" - $1,300.00; 6–7" - $2,300.00.

BARE FEET: 5" - $1,100.00; 6" - $1,200.00; 8–9" - $1,800.00; 10–11" - $2,700.00.

JOINTED ELBOWS: 5½–6" - $2,500.00; 9–10" - $3,500.00.

JOINTED ELBOWS AND KNEES: 4½–6½" - $3,500.00; 8–9" - $4,400.00.

MARKED S.F.B.J., UNIS, OR OTHER LATE FRENCH ALL BISQUE: 5–6" - $550.00; 7–8" - $700.00.

PAINTED EYES: 4–5" - $575.00; 7–8" - $900.00.

"WRESTLER": Fat legs, painted high top boots, glass eyes, closed or open mouth. Excellent bisque: 8" one-piece body and head - $1,000.00. Bare feet: 8" - $2,300.00; 11" - $3,200.00. Swivel neck, jointed shoulders and hips: 8" - $1,800.00.

PLATE 1

PLATE 2

PLATE 3

PLATE 1: 5½" French all bisque with slim body and limbs, kid lined at neck. Jointed neck, shoulders and hips. Painted-on long white stockings and multi-strapped boots. Glass set eyes, closed mouth and original clothes and wig. Shown with very old enameled French furniture. $2,200.00.

Plate 2: 7¼" French "wrestler" marked #102. Set glass eyes, original wig, pierced ears and painted-on high top boots. Kid-lined wood pegged joints at shoulders. Open mouth with two upper teeth. $1,800.00 up.

PLATE 3: 7¼" French "wrestler" shown with cloth and cardboard wardrobe and doll clothes. $2,600.00.

PLATE 4

PLATE 5

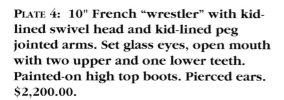

PLATE 4: 10" French "wrestler" with kid-lined swivel head and kid-lined peg jointed arms. Set glass eyes, open mouth with two upper and one lower teeth. Painted-on high top boots. Pierced ears. $2,200.00.

PLATE 5: 5" French all bisque dolls with slim bodies and limbs. Both have kid-lined swivel necks, jointed shoulders and hips and have set glass eyes and closed mouths. Both have stockings to knees and shoes with two straps. Original wigs and clothes. $2,000.00 each.

PLATE 6: 9" French "wrestler" shown nude. Original wig, pierced ears and open mouth with upper teeth. Set glass eyes. Shown for body detail, no price given.

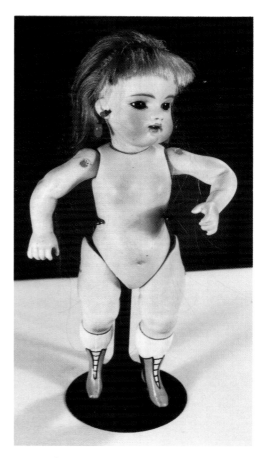

PLATE 6

PLATE 7

PLATE 7: 7" French all bisque with jointed neck, shoulders and hips. Painted-on high top boots and long white stockings. Left arm is bent and has excellent modeled hands. Glass eyes, feathered eyebrows, open/closed mouth. Marked "132" and looks very much like a miniature Bru. $2,300.00.

PLATE 8: A full-length view of a Bru-looking all bisque doll. Excellent detailed hands and high top boots.

PLATE 8

PLATE 9

PLATE 10

PLATE 11

PLATE 9: 7½" French-type all bisque with kid-lined swivel neck, jointed shoulders and hips. Sleep glass eyes, closed mouth and feathered eyebrows. Painted stockings to knees. Original wig and possibly original dress. $850.00.

PLATE 10: 8" French-type all bisque with set glass eyes, feathered heavy eyebrows, open mouth and painted white stockings to knees and strapped shoes with pom poms. Original wig and possibly original dress. $900.00.

PLATE 11: 8" French-type all bisque with slim legs, tan socks and black ankle strapped shoes. Set glass eyes, open/closed mouth, tiny multi-stroked eyebrows, and pierced ears. $900.00.

PLATE 12

PLATE 13

PLATE 14

PLATE 12: 3½" and 4½" French-type dolls. Both have swivel, kid-lined necks and are jointed at shoulders and hips. Set glass eyes, original wigs, closed mouths, and slim bodies. The tall one has original leather gloves and white painted stockings to knees. The small one has yellow boots with black toes and trim. $500.00 each.

PLATE 13: 4" French-type all bisque with swivel necks, jointed shoulders and hips, glass set eyes, and closed mouths. Painted-on socks and ankle strapped shoes. Both have original wigs and clothes. $500.00 each.

PLATE 14: 3" Chinese all bisque with swivel neck, jointed shoulders and hips. Molded-on hat and painted features. All original clothes. Black painted legs. May have been made in France. $650.00.

German All Bisque Dolls

It is quite possible that most of the fine quality German-made all bisque dolls came from the Kestner factory. Here are a few clues to known Kestners: the top lip is painted "squared off" at the ends, glossy multi-stroked eyebrows, upper and lower black eyeliner. Many have lower painted lashes only, but some will have upper painted lashes also. Kestner liked blue-grey eyes and used plaster pates. Shoes were generally black with yellowish soles and had one strap with a pom-pom on the toe. A great number of the dolls have white unpainted bisque socks with blue top band, but some will also be pink vertical ribbed with no top band or will have a rose or magenta band. Socks also used blue circular with no top bands and blue vertical ribbing with dark blue bands.

Mold numbers for Kestner-made all bisque dolls are: 112, 130, 142, 150, X150, 151, 152, 155, 164, 192, 208, 257, 307, 310, 314, 600, 620.

The German-made swivel heads strung without a wooden neck plug have holes at the sides of the neck and the head is strung with the arm rubber. The heads will not hold a turned position and will always snap back to face front.

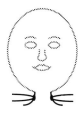

The quality of German-made all bisque dolls can vary a great deal. There can be some with excellent bisque and fine artist painting. These command the highest prices. Dolls can also be made with poor bisque and/or artist painting, and their prices are listed lower. "High" color usually will indicate that the doll was made in the late 1920's and 1930's.

SWIVEL NECK, GLASS EYES: Open or closed mouth, painted-on shoes and socks. Nicely dressed and no damage. 4" - $385.00; 5" - $465.00; 7" - $650.00; 9" - $975.00. Jointed knees or elbows: 6" - $2,000.00; 8" - $3,000.00.

SWIVEL NECK, PAINTED EYES: Open or closed mouth, painted shoes and socks. Nice clothes and undamaged. 2−3" - $250.00; 4−5" - $300.00; 7" - $425.00; 9" - $750.00.

ONE-PIECE BODY AND HEAD, GLASS EYES: Excellent bisque, open or closed mouth, good wig and nice clothes. No damage. 3" - $250.00; 4½−5½" - $300.00; 7" - $500.00; 8−9" - $700.00; 11" − $1,200.00.

ONE-PIECE BODY AND HEAD, PAINTED EYES: Open or closed mouth, excellent bisque. Nicely dressed, no damage and good wig or molded hair. 2" − $85.00; 3−4½" - $185.00; 6" - $250.00; 7−8" -$300.00; 11" - $950.00.

Marked 155, 156, 162, glass eyes: Smiling, open/closed or closed mouth, swivel head. 4½" - $500.00; 6" - $785.00; 9" - $900.00; 11" - $1,200.00.

Molded-on clothes or underwear: Jointed at shoulders and hips or shoulders only. No damage, nice clothes and wig. 4½" - $185.00; 5½" - $250.00; 6" - $300.00; 7" - $425.00.

Marked 100, 125, 225: Made by Alt, Beck & Gottschalck. One-piece body and head. Closed or open/closed mouth, glass eyes. No damage. 5" - $245.00; 6½" - $385.00; 8" - $550.00; 10" - $900.00.

Marked 150: Made by Kestner or Bonn. One-piece body and head, not damaged, nicely dressed, and wigged. 4" - $275.00; 6" - $385.00; 9" - $750.00; 11" - $1,000.00. Swivel neck and glass eyes: 5" - $500.00; 9" - $1,100.00; 11" - $1,500.00.

Molded Hair: One-piece body and head, no damage, nicely dressed. Excellent quality painting and bisque. 5" - $250.00; 6½" - $375.00.

Marked 886, 890: Made by Simon & Halbig or any all bisque marked with S&H. Painted-on high top boots with five straps. Nicely dressed and no damage. 6" - $975.00; 8" - $1,500.00.

Black or Brown All Bisque: Glass eyes, swivel head: 4–5" - $950.00; 7–8" - $1,200.00. One-piece body and head, glass eyes: 4–5" - $450.00; 7–8" - $675.00. Painted eyes, one-piece body and head: 5" - $250.00; 7" - $485.00. Swivel head: 5" - $450.00; 7" - $600.00.

Molded-on Hat or Bonnet: All in perfect condition. 6" - $450.00; 8" - $600.00.

Long Stockings: To above the knees. Glass eyes, open or closed mouth, jointed at neck. Stockings will be black, blue, or green. Prices based on being in perfect condition. 5½" - $625.00; 7¼" - $825.00.

Flapper: One-piece body and head, painted-on long stockings to above knees (usually yellowish color.) Long, thin limbs, fired-in color, one strap painted-on shoes. 5" - $325.00; 7" - $425.00. Same, but with molded hair: 5" - $300.00; 7" - $400.00. Same, but medium quality bisque and artist workmanship: 5" - $165.00; 7" - $250.00.

Marked with maker (S&H, JDK, ABG, etc.): Closed mouth, early excellent quality bisque, and character face. 7" - $1,200.00; 10" - $1,500.00. Same, but with open mouth and later quality bisque: 7" - $650.00; 10" - $1,100.00.

Pink Bisque: 1920's–1930's. Jointed shoulders and hips. Can have molded hair or wig. All in excellent condition. 3" - $80.00; 5" - $100.00; 7" - $185.00.

Photos on Page 15

Plate 15, 16: Facial detail and full body view of 8" extremely rare Kestner all bisque doll with "X" series style face. Swivel waist, delicate modeled hands, glass eyes. Very detailed tops to socks. This doll is valued at $2,300.00–2,500.00.

Plate 17, 18: Side view shows the detail of the cut pate, which is very "French," and the modeling to the hands. Back view shows stringing detail and neck modeling which defines this doll as a Kestner.

PLATE 15

PLATE 16

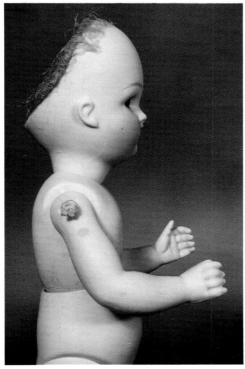

PLATE 17

PLATE 18

PLATE 19

PLATE 20

PLATE 21

PLATE 19: 4½" Kestner with glass eyes, closed mouth, swivel neck, and jointed at shoulders and hips. Painted-on ribbed pink socks and one strap shoes. 3" baby with jointed shoulders and hips shown in tiny carriage. 4½" Kestner - $285.00; 3" baby - $95.00.

PLATE 20: On the left is an 8" all bisque marked "208-13." Swivel neck, jointed shoulders and hips, glass eyes, closed mouth, painted-on shoes and socks. On the right is a 7½" all bisque doll marked "208/0 with glass eyes, open/closed mouth, painted teeth, swivel neck, and jointed shoulders and hips. Painted-on socks and shoes. 8" - $850.00; 7½" - $900.00.

PLATE 21: On the left is a 5" all bisque doll with very heavy eyebrows, glass sleep eyes, open mouth, swivel neck, and jointed shoulders and hips. Painted-on socks and boots. On the right is a 4½" doll with one-piece body, head and legs. Jointed at shoulders only. Painted features. Both dolls have original wigs. 5" - $465.00; 4½" - $185.00.

PLATE 22

PLATE 23

PLATE 22: 10" very round, "fat" face doll with glass eyes, open mouth, double chin on one-piece body and head. Jointed shoulders and hips. Painted-on white socks and shoes. Good hand detail, original wig. Made in Germany by Kestner. $1,000.00.

PLATE 23: 8½" all bisque with one-piece body and head, glass eyes, closed mouth, and feathered eyebrows. Long ribbed stockings and painted-on shoes. Delicate hand detail. Possibly original clothes. $875.00.

PLATE 24: On the left is a 7" German all bisque marked "154/8." One-piece body and head, sleep glass eyes, closed mouth, and original gloves. Painted-on ribbed socks and one strap shoes. On the right is a French-type all bisque with heavy feathered eyebrows, glass eyes, and open mouth with tiny upper teeth. Jointed shoulders and hips. Original dress but replaced wig. Painted stockings to knees and high top boots. 7" German - $500.00; French-type - $725.00.

PLATE 24

PLATE 25

PLATE 25: 6" Kestner with glass eyes, one-piece body and head, jointed shoulders and hips. Painted-on ribbed stockings and yellow boots. Original wig, possibly original clothes. Holds 1½" all bisque doll that is jointed at the shoulders and hips and is in original costume. $385.00.

PLATE 26: Back row: All bisque dolls, both have sleep eyes and are marked "130." Jointed shoulders and hips. The one on the left is 7"; on the right, 6½". Front row: On the left is an Oriental with slanted glass eyes, painted-on shoes, swivel neck, and braid on back of head. On the right is a 3¾" doll marked "208." Swivel neck, painted eyes, and painted-on high top boots. 7" - $500.00; 6½" - $500.00; Oriental - $725.00; 3¾" - $300.00.

PLATE 26

PLATE 27

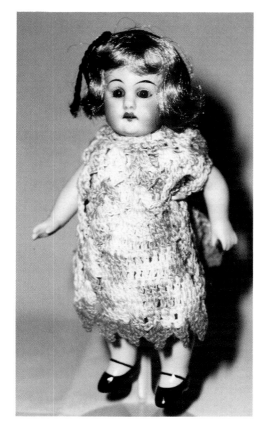

PLATE 28

PLATE 27: 7" closed mouth with glass eyes and original clothes. One-piece body and head, painted-on shoes and socks. Marked "Made in Germany/P43." $500.00.

PLATE 28: 8" all bisque marked "193-19/0/DEP." Made in Germany. Open mouth and glass eyes, painted-on shoes and socks. One-piece body and head. $700.00.

PLATE 29: 8" all bisque marked "83/150/18." Made by Kestner in Germany. Open/closed mouth, sleep glass eyes, molded-on shoes and socks. $600.00.

PLATE 29

PLATE 30

PLATE 31

PLATE 32

PLATE 30: 4" pugged nose all bisque boy and girl with one-piece body and head. Jointed shoulders and hips, painted-on knee high socks and strap shoes. Original wig and clothes. Glass eyes and closed mouth. Marked "137" on heads; "Germany" on backs. Each - $265.00.

PLATE 31: 3½" girl and boy that are all original. Girl is marked "132" and boy "182." Both are marked "Germany" on backs. Set glass eyes, one-piece body and head. Jointed at shoulders and hips, painted-on shoes and socks. Girl - $265.00; Boy - $385.00.

PLATE 32: 4" all bisque with one-piece body and head, pin-jointed at shoulders and hips. Painted features and has wig. All original "pregnant" clothes and has black and brown painted-on shoes with white socks. $245.00.

PLATE 33

PLATE 33: Seven tiny ¾" all bisque dolls with painted features and boots. One-piece bodies and heads, molded hair, and all original. Includes both boys and girls. Each - $85.00.

PLATE 34: Tiny 2" all bisque dolls, one kneeling and one standing. Each is jointed at shoulders only, has painted features, and all original. Marked "Germany." Each - $90.00.

PLATE 34

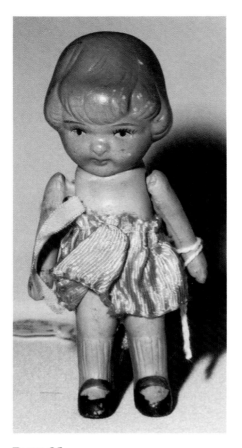

PLATE 35

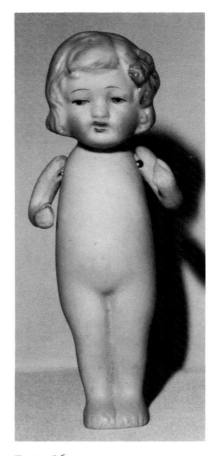

PLATE 36

PLATE 35: 3½" painted bisque with one-piece body and head, made in Germany. Painted-on shoes and socks, original skirt. $95.00.

PLATE 36: 6" all bisque with open/closed mouth, jointed shoulders only, and bent arms. $250.00.

PLATE 37: 4" all bisque doll with one-piece body and head. Painted features, pin jointed. Has molded-on black shoes with painted-on blue socks. Marked "11245/Germany." $200.00.

PLATE 37

German All Bisque Babies and Character Dolls

Prices are for excellent workmanship to the painting and quality of the bisque. There should be no chips, cracks, or breaks. Dolls can be dressed or nude. All bisque babies can date from 1900 with bent limb babies after 1906.

BABY, JOINTED NECK, SHOULDERS AND HIPS: Can have glass eyes or painted eyes; wigs or painted hair. 3½" - $185.00; 6" - $300.00; 8½" - $450.00.

BABY, JOINTED AT SHOULDERS AND HIPS ONLY: Well-painted features, free-formed thumbs and many have molded bottle in hand. Some have molded-on clothes. 3½" - $95.00; 6" - $185.00.

CHARACTER BABY: Jointed shoulders and hips, molded hair, painted eyes, character face. 4" - $185.00; 6" - $400.00. Glass eyes: 4" - $450.00; 6" - $550.00. Swivel neck, glass eyes: 6" - $600.00; 10" - $1,200.00 up.

TODDLER: Jointed neck, glass eyes, perfect condition. 7" - $700.00; 9" - $1,000.00; 11" - $1,600.00.

CANDY BABIES: Can be either German or Japanese. Generally poorly painted with high bisque color. Were given away at candy counters with purchase during the 1920's. 4" - $60.00; 6" - $80.00.

PINK BISQUE BABY: Jointed at shoulders and hips only, painted features and hair, bent baby legs. 1920's and 1930's. 2" - $50.00; 4" - $75.00; 8" - $135.00.

CHARACTER CHILD: Lifelike face or unusual in some manner. Glass eyes, swivel head: 5" - $500.00; 8½ − 9" - $1,200.00. Glass eyes, one-piece body and head: 5" - $375.00; 8½ − 9" - $785.00. Painted eyes, swivel head: 5" - $350.00; 8½ − 9" - $725.00. Painted eyes, one-piece body and head: 5" - $300.00; 9" - $675.00.

BABY BO-KAYE: Made by Alt, Beck & Gottschalck. Marked with mold number "1394." 4½" - $1,275.00; 6½" - $1,675.00.

BABY PEGGY (MONTGOMERY): Made by Louis Amberg and marked with paper label. 6" - $550.00.

BONNIE BABE: Made by Georgene Averill. Has paper label. 5" - $750.00; 7" - $1,000.00. Molded-on clothes: 6" - $1,300.00.

BYE-LO BABY: Made by J.D. Kestner. Has paper label. Jointed neck, glass eyes, solid dome. 4" - $525.00; 6" - $700.00. Jointed neck, wig, glass eyes: 5" - $700.00. Painted eyes, molded hair, one-piece body and head: 5" - $385.00; 6 − 8" - $650.00.

CAMPBELL KID: Molded-on clothes, Dutch-style hairdo. 5" - $285.00.

CHI CHI: Made by Orsini. Glass eyes: 5–6" - $1,600.00. Painted eyes: $950.00.

CHIN CHIN: Made by Heubach. 4½" - $325.00. Poor quality: 4½" - $250.00.

DIDI: Made by Orsini. Glass eyes: 5-6" - $1,700.00. Painted eyes: $950.00.

GERMAN FRENCH-TYPE: Marked "Germany" but has French slim limbs or other French features. 3½ – 4" - $500.00; 7–8" - $850.00.

GOOGLY: 1911 on. Glass eyes: 6" - $650.00 up. Painted eyes: 4" - $300.00 up; 6" - $485.00 up. Glass eyes, swivel neck: 6" - $775.00 up; 8" - $1,200.00 up. Jointed elbows and/or knees: 6" - $2,100.00; 7½" - $2,400.00. Marked with maker: (Example: K*R) 6½ – 7" - $2,600.00 up.

GRUMPY BOY: Marked "Germany." 4" - $185.00. (See also under "Japanese All Bisque.")

HAPPIFATS: Boy or girl. 5" - $365.00 each.

HEBEE OR SHEBEE: 4½" - $450.00 each.

LITTLE IMP: Has hoofed feet. 6½" - $600.00.

MIBS: Made by Louis Amberg. Could be marked "1921" on back and have paper label with name. 3½" - $250.00; 5" - $375.00.

OUR FAIRY: Molded hair and painted eyes. 9" - $1,600.00. Wig and glass eyes: 9" - $1,900.00.

OUR MARY: Has paper label. 4½" - $475.00.

PEEK-A-BOO: By Drayton. 4" - $325.00.

PETERKIN: 9" - $450.00.

QUEUE SAN BABY: Various poses. 5" - $300.00. (See also under "Japanese All Bisque.")

SCOOTLES: Made for Cameo. 6" - $950.00.

SONNY: Made by Averill. 5" - $850.00.

TYNIE BABY: Made for Horsman. Glass eyes: 9" - $1,700.00. Painted eyes: 9" - $1,100.00.

VEVE: Made by Orsini. 6" - $1,700.00.

WIDE AWAKE DOLL: 7½" - $325.00. (See also under "Japanese All Bisque.")

PLATE 38

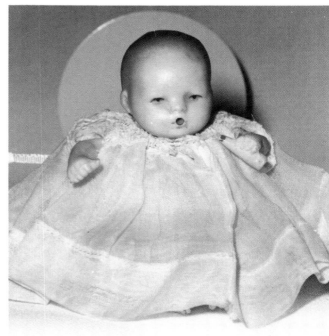

PLATE 39

PLATE 38: 8" and 9" all bisque babies by Kestner,
marked "B Made in 8/Germany." Both have sleep eyes
and open/closed mouth with molded tongue. Kid-lined
neck socket. Both have original wigs. The 8" doll's
clothes are original. 8" - $950.00; 9" - $1,000.00.

PLATE 39: 4" bent limb baby with one-piece body and
head. All original. Open mouth and has modeled bottle
in one hand. Baby is marked "821/9½/Germany."
$95.00.

PLATE 40: 3½" all original painted bisque bent limb
baby with open/closed mouth. Marked "158" on back.
Made in Germany, ca. 1930. $95.00.

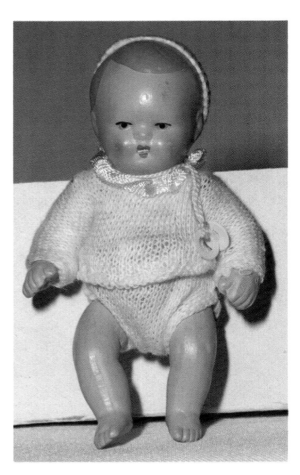

PLATE 40

PLATE 41

PLATE 42

PLATE 41: 9" all bisque "Tynie Baby" made for Horsman Doll Company. Sleep eyes, spray painted hair, and wears original dress. Marked "1924 by/E.I. Horsman Co. Inc./Made in Germany/38." $1,100.00.

PLATE 42: 8" all bisque Oriental baby with glass eyes, open mouth, and tiny sculptured teeth. All original clothes. Made in Germany by Kestner. $950.00.

PLATE 43: 5" all bisque "Bonnie Babe" made by Georgene Averill. All original. Open mouth with two lower teeth, sleep eyes, and molded hair. Painted-on shoes and socks. $750.00.

PLATE 43

PLATE 44

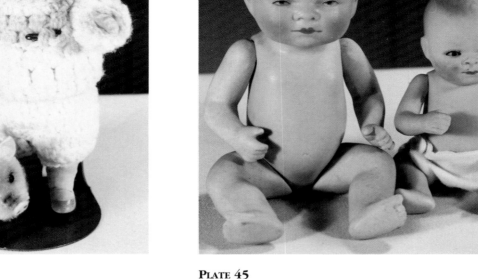

PLATE 45

PLATE 44: 6" "Bonnie Babe" with painted-on shoes and socks, open/closed lop-sided mouth with lower teeth, glass sleep eyes, and deeply modeled hair. Jointed at shoulders and hips. Made in Germany. $825.00.

PLATE 45: 6" all bisque "Bye-lo" with painted eyes and one-piece body and head. Shown with tiny 4" with swivel neck and glass eyes. Both are jointed at shoulders and hips. 6" - $400.00; 4" - $525.00.

PLATE 46: 6" all bisque "Bye-lo" with swivel neck, glass eyes, bare feet, and wig. Jointed at shoulders and hips. Original clothes. $750.00.

PLATE 46

PLATE 47

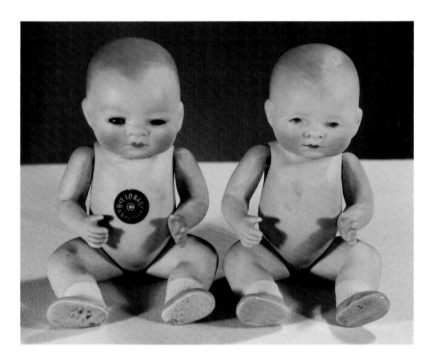

PLATE 48

PLATE 47: On the left is a 6" "Bye-lo" baby with swivel neck, glass eyes, and painted-on pink shoes. Shown on the right is a 5" "Bye-lo" with one-piece body and head and painted-on blue shoes. Both are jointed at shoulders and hips. 6" - $800.00; 5" - $675.00.

PLATE 48: Two 5" all bisque "Bye-lo" babies with painted-on shoes. Each doll has a one-piece body and head. Doll on the left has glass eyes and original paper label. Doll on the right has painted eyes. Both are jointed at shoulders and hips. Glass eyes - $625.00; Painted eyes - $525.00.

PLATE 49

PLATE 49: 8" "Bye-lo" baby with swivel neck, glass eyes, and wig that is all original. Doll is in original basket. Baby and basket - $900.00.

PLATE 50: 6" "Bye-lo" twins with sleep glass eyes and wigs. Each has a one-piece body and head. Jointed at the shoulders and hips only. Both are original in their original basket. Their wardrobe is stored under the dolls. Twins in basket - $1,250.00.

PLATE 50

PLATE 51

PLATE 52

PLATE 53

PLATE 51: 6" twin all original "Bye-lo" babies with one-piece body and head and painted features. Jointed at shoulders and hips only. Shown in their original flannel and lace sacque. Twins - $895.00.

PLATE 52: 6" "Bye-lo" with painted features and one-piece body and head. Original ivory painted bed and bed coverings. $525.00

PLATE 53: Three china glazed "Bye-lo" salt and pepper shakers, 1½" and 3" sizes. All are on round bases that hold the cork insert. In the foreground is a 3½" "Bye-lo" porcelain figurine with painted features. It is in a "roll over" position and will not lay flat. 1½" shaker - $145.00; 3" shaker - $265.00; 3½" figurine - $265.00.

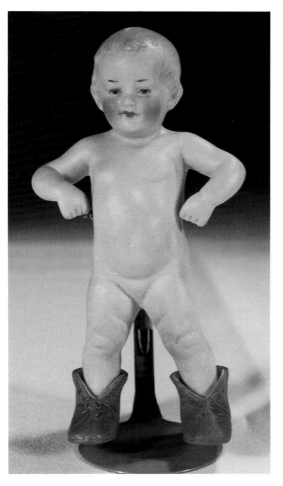

PLATE 54

PLATE 55

PLATE 54: 5" "muscle boy" figure with modeled-on boots, molded hair, and painted features. Excellent modeling details. Made in Germany. $265.00.

PLATE 55: On the left is a 4" figure with painted features, wide open/closed mouth as if yelling. Wide spread legs with painted-on shoes. Came in one-piece cotton romper suit. Shown on the right is a 4" figure with outstretched arms, modeled hair, painted features and shoes. Both are made in one piece. Yelling figure - $265.00; Outstretched arms figure - $200.00.

PLATE 56

PLATE 56: Left: 3½" boy with modeled hair coming far down on forehead, large painted eyes to side and only jointed at shoulders. Marked "174/2." Middle: One-piece sitting figure with molded hair, eyes painted far to side, open/closed mouth, and painted teeth. Marked "556" on back. Right: Little girl that is pair to boy shown on left. Eyes painted toward boy when placed side-by-side. Also marked "174/2." Boy or girl, each - $245.00; Sitting figure - $265.00.

PLATE 57

PLATE 58

PLATE 59

PLATE 57: 3" baby with one-piece body and head, painted features, and original clothes. Marked "6/0 Germany." Shown in all celluloid baby buggy. 3" baby - $165.00; Buggy - $125.00.

PLATE 58: 9" laughing boy character that is marked "790-6." Original crocheted one-piece suit. Painted-on shoes and socks. Mouth is open/closed, eyes are painted, and hair is painted brown. Made in Germany. $600.00.

PLATE 59: On the left is a 4" figurine with one-piece body and head. The mouth is opened wide and hands are molded into fists. Original clothes. Unmarked, possibly made in Germany. Shown on the right is a 4" figurine with molded-on clothes. Pin-jointed shoulders, one-piece body, head, and legs. Unmarked, possibly made in Japan. 4" on left - $185.00; 4" on right - $140.00.

PLATE 60

PLATE 61

PLATE 60: 5½" and 3½" boys with molded-on clothes and painted-on black shoes. One-piece bodies and heads, pin-jointed at shoulders and hips. Made in Germany. 5½" - $250.00; 3½" - $160.00.

PLATE 61: 4" and 3½" figures with one-piece bodies and heads and molded-on clothes. Both have pin-joints at shoulders and hips. Both are marked "Germany." Additional marks on the legs of the 4" doll are "3/0" and "30." 4" - $185.00; 3½" - $160.00.

PLATE 62: 8", 5¾", and 4¼" boys with molded-on clothes. All have "pouty" looks and have one-piece body and heads. All have pin-jointed shoulders and hips. Made in Germany. 8" - $450.00; 5¼" - $265.00; 4¼" - $200.00.

PLATE 62

PLATE 63

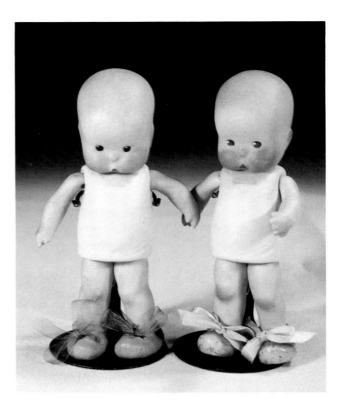

PLATE 64

PLATE 65

PLATE 63: 4" sitting girl with molded-on shirt, painted features, and mohair wig. Both arms are modeled away from the body. Made in Germany. Shown with 2½" sitting boy with modeled-on helmet, pants, and painted strap. The wings are fired onto the body. Marked ♔N. Girl - $195.00; Boy - $425.00.

PLATE 64: 4" "Hee-be and She-be" with one-piece body and head. Arms and legs are strung and shoes are painted-on with holes to allow ribbon to be tied through them. Painted features. Made in Germany for Horsman Doll Company. Each - $450.00.

PLATE 65: On the left is 5" "Snow Boy" that has painted features, dimples and smile. Pebble-textured clothes and hat. Made in Germany. Shown on the right is 5" boy with molded-on clothes. Marked "3132 Germany." Both dolls have one-piece body and head that is jointed at shoulders and hips. 5" "Snow Boy" - $265.00; 5" boy - $325.00.

PLATE 66

PLATE 67

PLATE 66: 3½" Santa Claus figures. Their jointed necks allow the entire head and beard to move from side to side. Both have holes in their hands for holding a small bag or tree. The Santa on the left has painted features. Left - $160.00; right - $185.00.

PLATE 67: 2½", 1½", and 1" brown all bisque figures made in one piece. All have painted features and molded-on clothes. Baby is modeled as part of the cradle. All are marked "Germany." 2½" - $125.00; 1½" - $95.00; 1" - $100.00.

PLATE 68: 4¾" and 2" "Annie Roonie" dolls with molded-on clothes and painted features. The smaller doll is missing her yarn wig. Jointed at shoulders only. Both came in various color dresses. Made in Germany. 4¾" - $375.00; 2" - $225.00.

PLATE 68

PLATE 69

PLATE 70

PLATE 71

PLATE 69: 4" with molded-on bonnets, molded hair and one-piece body, legs, and head. Pin-jointed at shoulders. Doll in pink hat has unusual hairdo. The blue hat version has molded-on scarf. Pink hat - $300.00; Blue hat - $300.00.

PLATE 70: Original 5½" "Little Boy Blue" with metal horn on chain. Painted features, molded hair. Jointed at shoulders and hips only. Painted-on shoes and socks. Marked "170/5." $400.00.

PLATE 71: 7½" boy and girl with molded hair, painted features, and painted-on shoes and socks. All original. Girl has molded bows. Dolls marked "B-85 Germany." Boy - $300.00; Girl - $325.00.

PLATE 72

PLATE 73

PLATE 72: 2" and 4½" with one-piece body and heads and original clothes. Molded hair, painted features. The larger doll is marked "805-2" on its back. It has ribbed stockings and strap shoes. The 2" doll has painted-on black boots. 2" - $95.00; 4½" - $265.00.

PLATE 73: 6" that looks like she was made in Japan but is marked "665 B/Germany/15." Wears original three layered crepe paper dress. Jointed shoulders only. $125.00.

PLATE 74: 3", 3½", and 4" all bisque dolls with one-piece bodies and heads; jointed shoulders and hips. All have painted features. Shoes and socks are painted on. The three dolls in the background were made in Germany and have molded hair. The doll in the foreground has painted hair and was made in Japan. German dolls - $185.00; Japan-made doll - $60.00.

PLATE 74

PLATE 75

PLATE 76

PLATE 77

PLATE 75: 5" and 3" "Flappers" with slightly turned heads, painted features, and original wigs. Both have painted-on mid-thigh stockings and heeled shoes. They have one-piece bodies and heads with jointed shoulders and hips. The 5" doll has original clothes and is marked "120/2." The smaller doll is marked "129." 5" - $365.00; 3" - $185.00.

PLATE 76: 2" and 4½" "Flapper" dolls that are both original. Both have molded hair with holes to tie ribbons and painted features. They have one-piece bodies and turned heads. Jointed at shoulders and hips. The smaller one has unpainted legs and painted high heel shoes. The larger doll has painted mid-thigh stockings and heeled shoes. 2" - $150.00; 4½" - $300.00.

PLATE 77: 5½" black all bisque doll with swivel neck and jointed shoulders and hips. Glass eyes, closed mouth, and all original with original suitcase. Marked "J6 Germany 8" and possibly made by Kestner. Shown with unmarked 3" very black all bisque doll with glass eyes, wig, and one-piece body and head. Jointed at shoulders and hips. 5½" - $800.00; 3" - $165.00.

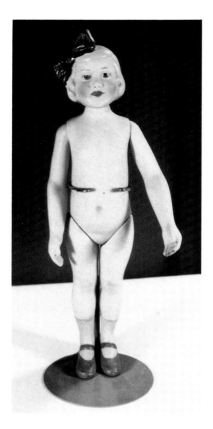

PLATE 78

PLATE 79

PLATE 78: 9" all bisque character girl with molded hair and bow, painted eyes, and open/closed mouth. Head fits down onto body in a very unusual manner and is jointed to move. Painted-on shoes and socks with rather large feet. Jointed at shoulders and hips. Supposedly designed and made by man who worked for Gebruder Heubach. His name "IGODI" is marked on doll. $1,200.00.

PLATE 79: 5" "DiDi" all bisque doll marked "11.0.1920/47" on head. Paper label on torso reads "DiDi/Regd. U.S. Pat. Off./Copr. 10-20 J.I. Orsini/Pat. Applied For." Has open/closed mouth with tiny sculptured teeth. Tiny sleep eyes, original wig, painted-on shoes. Index finger of right hand pointed while the rest of the fingers are curled. Original one-piece suit is shown pulled down to reveal paper label. $1,700.00.

PLATE 80: 5" dolls with glass eyes, closed mouth, and swivel necks. On the left is a French-type with original wig, feathered eyebrows, and kid-lined peg jointing. On the right is a character face doll with original wig and dress. She is marked "B 607/3." French-type - $575.00; Character - $500.00.

PLATE 80

PLATE 81

PLATE 81: 5 wonderful character all bisque dolls. All are 4" tall and made in one piece. They have glass eyes, mohair wigs, open/closed mouths, and modeled-on shirt tops. Finger and toe detail is excellent as is the quality of bisque. Each holds a different item: binoculars, butterfly, ball, bug, and cup. Made in Germany. Each - $500.00.

PLATE 82: 7" Orsini type doll marked "156/7." Excellent quality. Has glass eyes, open/closed mouth, and painted teeth. Original clothes and wig. Jointed at shoulders and hips. Hands are "star" shaped with second and third fingers molded together. Flesh-toned wash added to top of hands. Painted-on shoes and socks. $1,300.00.

PLATE 82

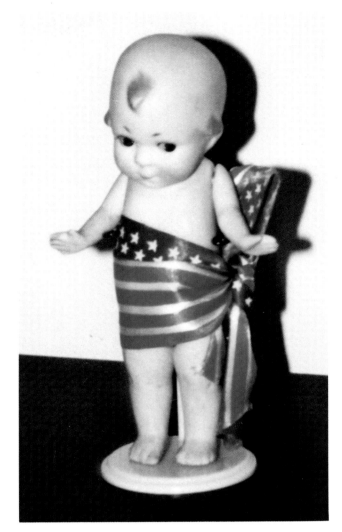

PLATE 83

PLATE 83: 5" character doll that is jointed at shoulders and hips. Has three molded tuffs of hair. (Some dolls have one tuff on the back of the head.) Marked "10883/Germany." $375.00.

PLATE 84: 6" "Veve" made by Orsini. All bisque with glass eyes, open/closed mouth, upper and lower teeth. Painted-on shoes and socks. May be original costume. 6" - $1,700.00.

PLATE 84

PLATE 85

PLATE 85: 5" all bisque "September Morn" designed by Grace Drayton. Deeply modeled hair, googly painted eyes to side and "O"-shaped tiny open/closed mouth. Feet molded into "water" base. Made in Germany. $385.00.

PLATE 86

PLATE 86: 5" "Our Fairy" with round paper seal on stomach. Glass googly eyes to side, original wig, and bare feet. One-piece body, head, and legs. Jointed shoulders only. Open/closed mouth with molded teeth. Made in Germany. $700.00.

PLATE 87

PLATE 88

PLATE 89

PLATE 87: On the left is a 5½" googly with painted eyes and one-piece body and head. Has jointed shoulders and hips. Painted-on shoes and socks, original wig. Holds tiny ½" all bisque doll that is jointed at hips and shoulders. On the right is a 4½" googly marked "292-10." Glass eyes are to the side. Jointed neck, shoulders, and hips. Painted-on shoes and socks, original wig. 5½" - $365.00; ½" - $35.00; 4½" - $450.00.

PLATE 88: 7", 5", and 3½" "Campbell Kid" figures with molded-on clothes and hair. Jointed shoulders only. Made for Horsman Doll Co. between 1912 and 1917. Made in Germany. 7" - $465.00; 5" - $285.00; 3½" - $195.00.

PLATE 89: 4½" googly with glass eyes and original wig. Marked "711/0." Painted-on shoes and socks. Extra joints at elbows and knees. $1,000.00.

PLATE 90

PLATE 91

PLATE 92

PLATE 90: On left is 4½" "Wide Awake" doll with molded-on Turkish style hat. Jointed at shoulders only and has bare feet. Marked "Germany." Shown with 3½" mad-looking sailor boy molded in one piece with boat modeled between legs. Molded-on clothes. Made in Germany. "Wide Awake" - $225.00; Sailor - $200.00.

PLATE 91: In the background is a 4½" "Chubby" that is jointed at the shoulders only. Very detailed and well-modeled underclothes with ruffle around legs. 6" "Chubby" with paper label on chest and jointed at shoulders only. Excellent quality bisque and modeling. Marked "1. W & C." In foreground is a 3" "Chubby" with molded hair and 4" with wig. Both are jointed at shoulders only. Both have very detailed hands and painted-on underclothes. Both have "worried" painted eyebrows. All were made in Germany. 4½" - $225.00; 6" - $450.00; 3" - $200.00; 4" - $200.00.

PLATE 92: 5" "O You Kid" with paper label on stomach and painted-on full pajama suit. Modeled hair with part of ears exposed, googly eyes to side. Jointed at neck only. Made in Germany. $550.00.

PLATE 93

PLATE 94

PLATE 95

PLATE 96

PLATE 93: 4½" "Happifats" with modeled-on under-wear. On left is a boy with v-necked one-piece painted-on underwear. Molded hair. The other two are girls with shoulder strapped, panty-style outfits. Molded curled hair. All made in Germany. Girls - $365.00 each; Boy - $365.00.

PLATE 94: Dressed 4½" "Happifat" boy and girl that are jointed at shoulders only. Clothes are molded on, features are painted. Made in Germany. Boy and girl - $365.00 each.

PLATE 95: 5½" "Wide Awake" doll with one-piece body, head, and legs. Jointed at shoulders only. Painted-on shoes and socks. Marked "103851/Germany." Shown with 5" marked "Wide Awake Doll/Registered Germany. Jointed shoulders and hips, bare feet. 5½" - $265.00; 5" - $300.00.

Plate 96: 5½" and 4" googlies. Larger figure is shoulder jointed and has molded dagger with painted belt. 4" figure is pin jointed and has molded-on boots. Both have separate movable bisque hats that are strung to the arms. Both are made in Germany. 5½" - $425.00; 4" - $300.00.

Japanese All Bisque

Japan poured out thousands of all bisque dolls during the 1920's and 1930's. They can range from very poor quality to excellent quality. They generally will be figures with no moving parts called "immobiles" or figures jointed at the shoulders only. Occasionally, collectors will find multi-jointed Japan figures.

Prices are for good quality bisque, good artist painting, and the doll being in good condition with no chips, breaks, or cracks. Small paint wear is not important unless it is the painted features of the doll's face.

BENT LEG BABY: May or may not be jointed at hips and shoulders. Very good quality bisque: 3½–5" - $20.00–75.00. Medium to poor quality: 3½–5" - $6.00–45.00. Toddler: Same as baby but on toddler body, jointed at hips. 3½–5" - $35.00–90.00.

"BETTY BOOP" STYLE: Bobbed hair, large painted eyes to side, and one-piece body and head. 4" - $30.00; 7" - $50.00.

CANDY BABIES: See listing under "German All Bisque Babies and Character Dolls."

CHILD WITH MOLDED CLOTHES: 4½" - $45.00; 6" - $60.00.

COMIC CHARACTERS: Our Gang: 3½" - $80.00–90.00. Snow White: 5½" - $100.00. Dwarfs: 2½–3" - $100.00 each.

GRUMPY BOY: Marked "Japan." 4" - $85.00.

IMMOBILES: Figurines, no joints. Children: 3" - $45.00; 5" - $50.00. Indians: 3" - $70.00; 5" - $95.00. Dutch children: 2½–3" - $35.00; 5" - $45.00. Santa Claus: 3½–4" - $95.00. Adults: 5" - $75.00; 7" - $95.00.

MARKED NIPPON: 4" - $40.00; 6" - $85.00.

OCCUPIED JAPAN: 3½" - $20.00; 5" - $30.00; 7" - $45.00.

QUEUE SAN BABY: Various poses. 4" - $85.00–100.00.

WIDE AWAKE DOLL: 7½" - $125.00.

PLATE 97: 5½" "Betty Boop" type figure, made in Japan. Jointed at shoulders only. $40.00.

PLATE 97

PLATE 98: 8" "Betty Boop" type all bisque figure, that is jointed at shoulders only. Made in Japan. $65.00.

PLATE 98

PLATE 99

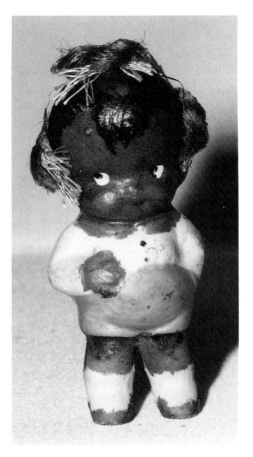

PLATE 100

PLATE 101

PLATE 99: 5" immobile made in Japan. Girl figure has hole in her hand to hold flowers. $60.00.

PLATE 100: 2¾" black immobile with three tuffs of hair. Made in Japan. $35.00.

PLATE 101: A pair of 3" immobiles, made in Japan. Butler/waiter - $50.00; Girl holding flower - $45.00.

PLATE 102

PLATE 103

PLATE 102: 4" Dutch boy and girl immobiles. Dutch figures were very popular during the 1910's and 1920's. Made in Japan. Each - $40.00.

PLATE 103: Dutch water boy and girl immobiles. Each - $40.00.

PLATE 104: 5" and 3¾" bride and groom immobiles, made in Japan. Groom's glasses are painted on. Bride - $60.00; Groom - $75.00.

PLATE 104

PLATE 105

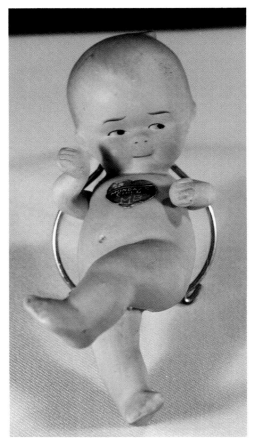

PLATE 106

PLATE 107

PLATE 105: 3" "Pudgy Doll" which is a Kewpie copy from Japan. These dolls can have blue, pink, or green wings. Finger and arms mold seams are not cleaned as well as the real Kewpies. No joints, heavy orange spray paint between legs. $85.00.

PLATE 106: 5" all bisque child in lazy, laying down position. Made all in one piece. Painted features and hair with "grumpy" painted eyebrows. Eyes painted to the side. Heart-shaped paper label is marked "Monday's Child/MB." Made by Morimura Brothers of Japan. $55.00.

PLATE 107: Pair of sitting down "Grumpy" dolls, made in Japan. One has molded hair; the other is wigged. Both are made in one piece and have closed fists. Molded hair - $45.00; Wigged - $50.00.

PLATE 108

PLATE 109

PLATE 108: 5" "Queue San Baby" marked also "Registered U.S. Patent" in diamond-shaped paper label. Has molded-on hat, painted features and shoes, and braided queue down its back. One-piece body and head; jointed shoulders and hip. Made in Japan. $100.00.

PLATE 109: 6" girl with painted-on molded hair and hair ribbon. Jointed at shoulders only. Head tilted downward and eyes painted to the side. Made in Japan. $65.00.

PLATE 110: 3" and 6" girls with molded hair. Both are jointed at shoulders only and have painted features. The 6" doll has bent elbows. The 3" doll has eyes painted to side. 3" - $35.00; 6" - $50.00.

PLATE 110

PLATE 111

PLATE 112

PLATE 111: 4" little boy from the 1910's. Molded-on romper, jointed at the shoulders only, and painted hair. $45.00.

PLATE 112: 4½" "Dream Baby" type made in Japan. Original christening gown made of muslin and ribbon. Jointed shoulders and hips.

PLATE 113: 6" child with molded hair and painted features. Eyes painted to side. Jointed shoulders only, legs modeled spread apart. Possibly original dress. Made in Japan. $75.00.

PLATE 113

PLATE 114

PLATE 115

PLATE 114, 115: 5" bisque head with two faces – one crying, one asleep. Painted features, spray painted hair. All original. Body and limbs are made of stone bisque. Made in Japan. $100.00.

PLATE 116: On the left is a painted 1½" bisque baby marked "Japan LL" and stamped "Japan." 1920's or 1930's. Shown with a 3½" baby made of unpainted bisque. Marked with triangle in circle. Made in Japan. 1½" - $20.00. 3½" - $35.00.

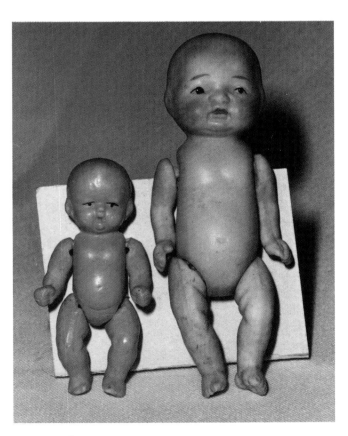

PLATE 116

PLATE 117

PLATE 117: 5" and 2" bent leg babies that are jointed at shoulders and hips. Both may be "Bye-lo" copies. 5" - $95.00; 2" - $50.00.

PLATE 118: 8" character girl from 1920's, made in Japan. Unusual in size. One-piece body and head, molded hair, and painted features. Open/closed mouth with painted teeth. $165.00.

PLATE 118

PLATE 119

PLATE 119: 5" and 3½" sailor boys with one-piece head and bodies. Molded-on clothes and pin-jointed. Both are marked "Japan." 5" - $55.00; 3½" - $35.00.

PLATE 120: 3¾" one-piece body, head, and legs. Pin-jointed shoulders. Bisque hat is separate and attached by string so it moves around the head. Marked "Japan." $50.00.

PLATE 120

Half Dolls

Half dolls have been included in this album of dolls because so many are made of all bisque, as well as china glaze figures. Half dolls are very difficult to price due to the many different kinds of dolls and the quality of material and workmanship. Half dolls can vary within the same mold casing because the quality of workmanship ranges from poor to excellent. They must be evaluated on a one-to-one basis. Each one is so different that the prices can vary greatly. The only guideline is the following listing that places the "types" into categories. Remember, a guide is just that – a guide of price ranges. Each item may be priced within this range. Prices reflect artisan quality on each piece. If quality is less than excellent expect "lower than book" prices. Items that are unusual or have exceptional quality will be priced higher. Prices in this album are for undamaged figures with no chips, cracks, or missing fingers.

ARMS AND HANDS COMPLETELY AWAY FROM FIGURE: Marked "Gobel," "Dressel, Kister & Co." China or bisque. 5" - $250.00 up; 8" - $425.00; 12" - $900.00.

ARMS EXTENDED, BUT HANDS ATTACHED TO FIGURE: China or bisque: 3" - $65.00; 5" - $75.00; 8" - $95.00. Papier maché or composition: 4½" - $30.00; 6½" - $70.00.

JOINTED SHOULDERS: China or bisque: 5" - $100.00; 8" - $125.00; 12" - $165.00. Papier maché: 4" - $35.00; 7" - $165.00. Wax over papier maché or composition: 4" - $40.00; 7" - $100.00.

CHILDREN OR MEN: 3" - $50.00 up; 5" - $75.00 up. Jointed shoulders: 6½–7" - $165.00 up.

COMMON FIGURES WITH ARMS AND HANDS ATTACHED TO FIGURE: China or bisque: 3" - $30.00; 5" - $40.00; 8" - $55.00; 12" - $95.00. Papier maché: 4" - $30.00, 7" - $45.00. Wax over papier maché or composition: 4" - $30.00; 7" - $45.00.

MARKED JAPAN, NIPPON, OR OCCUPIED JAPAN: 3" - $20.00; 5" - $30.00; 7" - $50.00.

PLATE 122

PLATE 121

PLATE 121: 5" half doll with extremely fine artist workmanship from the 1920's. The folded hands are away from the body. $400.00.

PLATE 122: Half doll with gray hair and applied flowers in hand and hair. Both arms modeled away from figure, excellent facial details. Made by Dressel, Kister & Co. in Germany. $500.00.

PLATE 123: Large half doll with older adult face. Comb in hair, large bust, both arms away from body. Holds rose in one hand. $525.00.

PLATE 123

PLATE 124

PLATE 125

PLATE 126

PLATE 124: Very unusual Dressel, Kister & Co. half doll with both arms modeled away from body. One hand is cupped at hip. Modeled-on cap, dark hair, and very detailed. Made in Germany. $575.00.

PLATE 125: This half figure, called "The Love Letter," has both arms away from body and a downcast appearance. Marked "Dressel, Kister & Co." $525.00.

Plate 126: 5" half doll with very wide base and arms modeled away from body. Holds flower and has flower in hairbow. Modeled-on clothes. $375.00.

PLATE 127

PLATE 128

PLATE 127: 4½" lady holding tennis racket. The painting of features and hair is only of fair quality. Made in Germany. $85.00.

PLATE 128: 3½" half doll with blue headband and holding a fan. Made in Germany. $70.00.

Plate 129: Beautiful German-made half doll with elaborate detail to hair decorations. Both arms away from body. Excellent face details. $600.00.

PLATE 129

PLATE 130

PLATE 131

PLATE 132

PLATE 130, 131: Half doll atop box of drawers and marked "Meissen." Skirt opens to reveal three drawers. It is 20" tall and 15" across the base. Wears original clothes. This item dates from the 1890's.

PLATE 132: Detail of half doll shows applied porcelain flowers on bonnet and very detailed hair. Both arms are modeled away from figures. $1,600.00.

PLATE 133

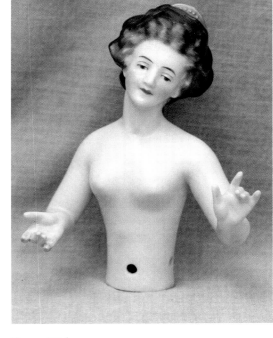

PLATE 134

PLATE 135

PLATE 133: 3¾" half doll with number "51" inside waist and "#22674" at waist. High piled brown hair with ribbon and molded bun. Very chunky arms and hands. $70.00.

PLATE 134: 5" half doll with Rudostalt mark inside base. On back of doll, marked in blue, "Made in Germany." Gold modeled-on crown, red line over eyes, nicely modeled brown hair. Glazed down to waist. Two center fingers curled. $675.00.

Plate 135: 6" half doll that could possibly be "Josephine." Has court appearance with feathers in hair. Marked with Gobel crown mark and "4." Both arms away from body. $575.00.

PLATE 136

PLATE 137

PLATE 138: 5½" Dressel, Kister & Co. half doll

PLATE 136: 5" half doll with the Richard Eckert & Co. mark. Her likeness could be of Anna Pavlova, a Russian ballerina. Molded necklace, bracelet, and flowers in hair. $585.00.

PLATE 137: 5" Dressel, Kister & Co. half doll with modeled-on purple hat. She holds a rose in her hand. Partly glazed, red line over eyes, and very elaborate hairdo with curl around neck. $550.00.

PLATE 138: 5½" Dressel, Kister & Co. half doll with molded lavender head scarf that fans out in back. Hair is modeled around the edge of the scarf. Molded eyelids, jointed arms, brush stroked eyebrows, and very serene expression. $675.00.

PLATE 138

PLATE 139: 5½" half doll with Gobel crown mark and incised "45.4." Molded eyelids and red lines over eyes. Original wig with sewn-in earrings. Delicate hands, arms modeled away from body. $500.00.

PLATE 139

PLATE 140: 4" half doll marked "52B80–" (Last number is unknown.) Original wig, jointed arms and open/closed mouth. Solid dome, molded eyelids, and very detailed breasts. $300.00.

PLATE 140

PLATE 141

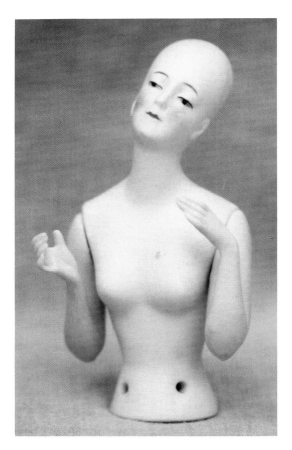

PLATE 142

PLATE 143

PLATE 141: 2½" half doll marked with number that is partly illegible (– – 87). Paper tag with her states "found in French warehouse." Blue bow in back of hairdo. Both arms modeled away from body. $175.00.

PLATE 142: 3½" half doll marked "#6078." Molded eyelids, ball-jointed shoulders, solid dome, and beautifully detailed ears and hands. $225.00.

PLATE 143: Child half doll with clown ruffle and hat. Made in Germany. $65.00.

PLATE 144

PLATE 145

PLATE 146

PLATE 147

PLATE 144: 3½" and 2½" half dolls with arms and hands attached to body. Both made in Germany. 3½" - $65.00; 2½" - $50.00.

PLATE 145: These 3" half dolls were made in Germany. The doll on the left has hands attached to body. The one on the right has both arms and hands attached. Left - $45.00; right - $35.00.

PLATE 146: Both half dolls were made in Germany. This particular model can come in a great many variations of clothing and hair ribbon colors. Also artist workmanship can vary. 4–5" - $35.00–$65.00.

PLATE 147: Both of these half dolls were made in Germany. The painting on left doll is splotchy but has good hand detail. 4" - $35.00; 3" - $50.00.

PLATE 148

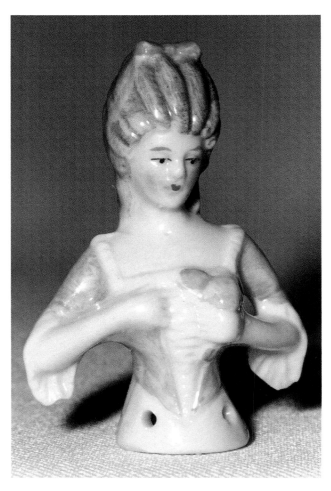

PLATE 149

PLATE 150: 1¼" tiny half doll with hands held like praying. Marked with number that is unreadable and "Germany." $35.00.

PLATE 149: 1¼" half doll with gray hair in sausage-style vertical curls. Marked "Germany." $35.00.

PLATE 150: Very nice half doll made in Germany with excellent detail and flared base. One hand is modeled away from body; the other is attached. Made by Dressel & Kister. Marked ⅄. 4" - $200.00.

PLATE 150

PLATE 151

PLATE 152

PLATE 151: 2½" half doll holding roses. Made in Germany and bears the number "5093½." $30.00.

PLATE 152: 2½" half doll with both hands attached to figure. Headband ribbon painted on. Made in Germany. $30.00.

PLATE 153: 3" half doll with both arms and hands attached to figure. Has painted beading in hair. Made in Germany. $30.00.

PLATE 153

PLATE 154

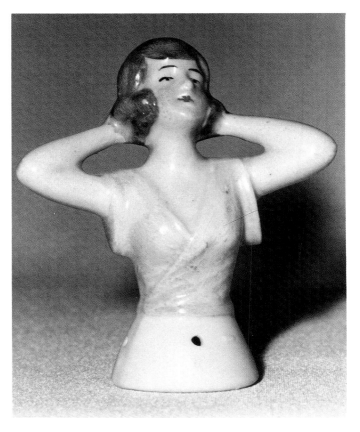

PLATE 155

PLATE 156

PLATE 154: 2½" half doll made in Germany and marked "1724." Elaborate detail to clothes and hat. $45.00.

PLATE 155: 2" half doll marked "13090" on back. Both hands attached to back of head. Made in Germany. $40.00.

PLATE 156: 4" half doll made in Germany with painted-on beads. Both arms attached to figure. $55.00.

PLATE 157

PLATE 158

PLATE 157: The half doll on the left was made in Germany; on the right, Japan. Both are 4" and have arms and hands attached to body. Germany - $65.00; Japan - $30.00.

PLATE 158: On the left is a tiny 1½" half doll holding a fan. Has a pink ribbon in her hair. Marked "6241/Germany." On the right is a half doll also holding a fan and/or flowers. She has an unusual top knot hairdo. Made in Japan. Germany - $35.00; Japan - $20.00.

PLATE 159: 2" half doll that looks like she was made in Japan, but is marked "Germany." Has shawl over shoulders. $25.00.

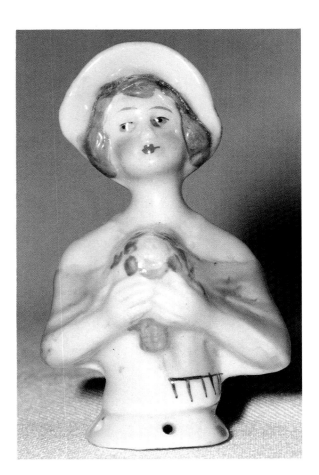

PLATE 159

PLATE 160

PLATE 161

PLATE 162

PLATE 160: 2" half doll made in Japan. Has red painted hair and holds roses. $20.00.

PLATE 161: 3" adult-faced half doll made in Japan with three long sausage curls in back and two over shoulders. Large nose. $40.00.

PLATE 162: 3" half doll, made in Germany. One hand is molded to hat and the other to hip. $65.00.

PLATE 163

PLATE 164

PLATE 163: Group of half dolls with unusual Oriental to the top row, left. All were made in Germany except for bright yellow top on bottom row, left. It was made in Japan. Japan - $35.00; Others - $65.00–125.00.

PLATE 164: Porcelain half dolls that are all flappers and made in Germany. Dolls on bottom row, left and right, have their arms molded to body. These two have the same style, but are a different size and color. $65.00–125.00.

PLATE 165

PLATE 166

PLATE 165: Fine grouping of half dolls. The doll on the top row, far left, is incised "Gobei 352. o." The doll next to her is marked with Gobel trademark and number "1806." The half doll on top row, center is 4½" tall and marked "8062." All were made in Germany. $350.00–600.00.

PLATE 166: This grouping of half dolls were made in Germany. The doll on the top row, far left, has a mohair wig. Also the doll on the top row, second from right, has an unusual collar. The two children on bottom row, right, are also unusual. The boy is a standing figure and the girl holds a vase. $300.00–550.00.

PLATE 167

PLATE 168

PLATE 167: 2" child half doll on pincushion base with jointed arms and molded headband. Made in Germany. $45.00.

PLATE 168: 2" half doll on pincushion base. Both arms are fully molded to body. Made in Japan. $30.00.

PLATE 169: This pincushion is 5" overall. The clown has a modeled-on neck ruffle and wears a white skull cap. Marked "France." $85.00.

PLATE 169

PLATE 170

PLATE 171

PLATE 172

PLATE 170: 2" half doll with dress over pincushion base. Made in Japan. $25.00.

PLATE 171: 5" half doll with sad, downcast head. Both arms and hands are modeled away from body. Attached to original pincushion base. Made in Germany. $300.00.

PLATE 172: Half doll with court-style hairdo on base marked "Made in Germany" in green circle along with "#11424," painted-on blue shoes, original skirt. 7" overall. $200.00.

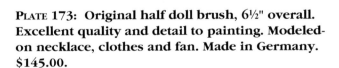

PLATE 173

PLATE 174

PLATE 173: Original half doll brush, 6½" overall. Excellent quality and detail to painting. Modeled-on necklace, clothes and fan. Made in Germany. $145.00.

PLATE 174: Half doll brush measuring 9" overall. (Half doll is 2½".) 1920's flapper, made in Japan. $125.00.

PLATE 175: Powder box with tennis player on lid. Marked "Made in France. Terre de Ratz." Although made of clay, it fits into the half doll collections. 6" overall. $325.00.

PLATE 175

PLATE 176

PLATE 177

PLATE 176: 2½" Dressel & Kister half doll holds rose and has rose in hair. Original shell lamp base on wire frame. 10" overall. $85.00.

PLATE 177: 6" baby head planter with applied lace porcelain flowers inside bonnet. Has molded loop for ribbon on top of bonnet. $45.00.

Plate 178: Although these heads are planters, they fit in well with dolls and many collectors like them. There are hundreds of variations, styles, and designs. The detail workmanship is usually very good to excellent. They are just a fun item to collect. $15.00 – 60.00.

PLATE 178

Kewpies

Kewpies were designed by Rose O'Neill and marketed from 1913. Kewpies can be identified by a paper label on its chest or by marks on the bottom of its feet or back. Prices are for undamaged items with no chips, cracks, or hairlines.

ONE-PIECE BODY AND HEAD: Jointed shoulders only. Blue wings, painted features with eyes to side. 1½" - $95.00; 2½" - $125.00; 4–5" - $165.00; 6" - $195.00; 7" - $250.00; 9" - $450.00; 12" - $1,400.00 up. With any article of clothing: 3" - $225.00; 5" - $250.00; 7" - $345.00; 9" - $600.00 up.

JOINTED AT HIPS AND SHOULDERS: 4" - $465.00; 9" - $875.00; 12" - $1,500.00 up.

ACTION KEWPIES:
CONFEDERATE SOLDIER: 5" - $700.00. **FARMER:** 4" - $495.00. **GARDENER:** 4" - $495.00. **GOVERNOR:** 4" - $450.00. **BRIDE AND GROOM:** 4" - $485.00. **GUITAR PLAYER:** 3½" - $400.00. **HOLDING PEN:** 3" - $385.00. **HOLDING CAT:** 4" - $500.00. **WITH BUTTERFLY:** 4" - $525.00. **WITH LADYBUG:** 4" - $525.00. **HUGGING:** 3½" - $300.00. **ON STOMACH:** (called "Blunderboo") 4" - $465.00; **THINKER:** 4" - $425.00. **TRAVELER:** With tan or black suitcase. 3½" - $325.00. **WITH BROOM/MOP:** 4" - $450.00. **WITH DOG, KEWPIEDOODLE:** 3½" - $1,500.00 up. **WITH HELMET:** 6" - $700.00. **WITH OUTHOUSE:** 2½" - $1,200.00. **WITH RABBIT:** 2½" - $400.00. **WITH ROSE:** 2" - $375.00. **WITH TEDDY BEAR:** 4" - $750.00. **WITH TURKEY:** 2" - $365.00. **WITH UMBRELLA:** 3½" - $450.00. **WITH UMBRELLA AND DOG:** 3½" - $1,400.00 up. **SOLDIER:** 4½" - $625.00. **SOLDIER AND NURSE:** 6" - $2,000.00. **IN BASKET WITH FLOWERS:** 3½" - $650.00. **IN DRAWSTRING BAG:** 4½" - $600.00. **BUTTONHOLE KEWPIE:** $165.00. **HOTTENTOT (BLACK KEWPIE):** 3½" - $400.00; 5" - $500.00. **PINCUSHION KEWPIE:** 2½" - $350.00. **KEWPIE'S DOG, DOODLE:** 1½" - $675.00; 3" - $1,200.00; 4–5" - $1,600.00.

BISQUE HEAD, PAINTED EYES, CLOTH BODY: 7" - $1,800.00; 10" - $2,200.00.

BISQUE HEAD, GLASS EYES, CLOTH BODY: 10" - $2,400.00; 12" - $2,700.00.

BISQUE HEAD, GLASS EYES, JOINTED TODDLER BODY: 10" - $4,200.00; 12" - $4,600.00; 16" - $6,500.00; 20" - $8,400.00.

ALL CLOTH, MASK FACE: Mint condition: 12" - $195.00; 15" - $300.00; 21" - $500.00; 26" - $1,000.00. Fair condition: 12" - $90.00; 15" - $125.00; 21" - $200.00; 26" - $350.00. Original clothes, mint: 12" - $285.00; 15" - $400.00; 21" - $675.00; 26" - $1,200.00.

CELLULOID KEWPIES: 2" - $50.00; 5" - $90.00; 9" - $175.00. Black: 5" - $135.00; 9" - $225.00. Jointed shoulders: 3" - $65.00; 5" - $95.00; 9" - $185.00.

PLATE 179

PLATE 180

PLATE 181

PLATE 179: Extremely well done "pigeon-toed" Kewpie cowboy that is attached to egg. 5" tall. $750.00 up.

PLATE 180: Kewpie's dog, Doodle. This 4" pet has wings and spots on nose. Extremely rare. $1,600.00.

PLATE 181: 1" Kewpie holding mandolin and 1½" Doodle. Both attached to 3½" log with hole in it. $725.00.

PLATE 182

PLATE 183

PLATE 182: 4" Kewpie with one-piece body, head, and legs. One has painted-on boots and the other has painted-on shoes and socks. Note how differently the eyes are painted. With boots -$250.00 ; With shoes -$200.00.

PLATE 183: 4¼" and 2¾" Kewpies. Both sitting and made in one piece. Large one has ladybug on foot. The smaller one has bug on its arms. 4¼" - $550.00; 2¾" - $300.00.

PLATE 184: Very large 7" "Thinker" Kewpie that is extremely well detailed and painted. Excellent quality. Shown with 5" standing Kewpie with jointed shoulders. Kewpie sticker on chest. "Thinker" - $585.00 up; 5" Kewpie - $165.00.

PLATE 184

PLATE 185

PLATE 186

PLATE 187

PLATE 185: 3½" sitting Kewpie in wicker chair. Arms are modeled crossed. One foot is resting atop the other. $500.00.

PLATE 186: 3" sitting Kewpie holding a well crafted black cat. $450.00.

PLATE 187: 3" Kewpie with open book on its lap. Head and upper body slightly twisted, as if ready to turn a page. $385.00.

PLATE 188

PLATE 189

PLATE 188: 3½" Kewpie holding mop. Mop bucket is attached on side of figure. $400.00.

PLATE 189: 3" sitting Kewpie holding pen and attached to glazed pen holder. Holder has worn gold trim. $465.00.

PLATE 190: 3" sitting Kewpie attached to handled basket. Marked on bottom of feet. $500.00.

PLATE 190

PLATE 191

PLATE 192

PLATE 191: 6", 7", and 8" all bisque Kewpies. All are jointed at shoulders only. Original ribbon around the far left Kewpie. $195.00 – 375.00.

PLATE 192: 6", 7", and 8" very rare Blind Kewpies. All are jointed at shoulders only. They were made by Kestner and sold this way with no eye detail. $375.00–685.00.

PLATE 193

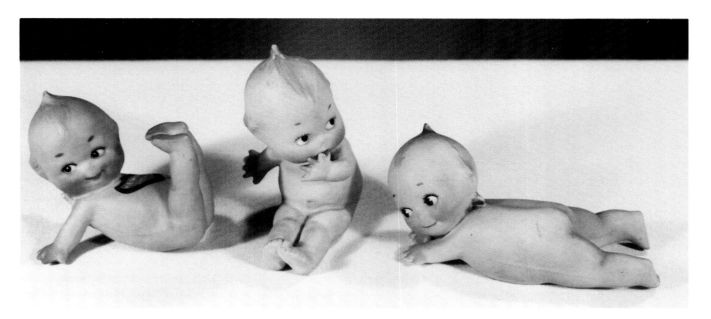

PLATE 194

PLATE 193: Seven Kewpies ranging from 3" to 6". All jointed at shoulders only. Ones with ribbons around them are original. Note that some of the paper Kewpie labels are attached to the ribbon. $150.00 – 200.00.

PLATE 194: Three Kewpies with tiny blue wings. The first two figures from the left are called "Blunderboo" Kewpies. The first one has Kewpie label on chest. The third figure is a Kewpie lying on its stomach. Note "Blunderboos" have a slightly different face and their eyes are painted differently. 4" - $465.00.

PLATE 195

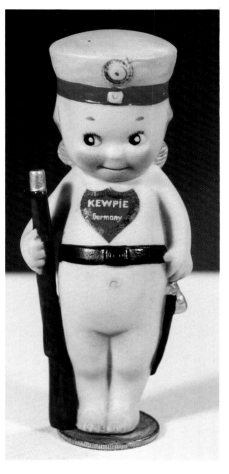

PLATE 196

PLATE 195: 4½" Bride and Groom Kewpies, all original. Her headpiece is made tight and cannot be moved back to show her face. Both have jointed shoulders only. Set - $500.00.

PLATE 196: 4" Kewpie soldier with rifle, belt, and saber sword. Very good quality. Has modeled-on gray hat with red hatband. $600.00.

PLATE 197: 3½" Kewpie holding guitar. Placement of hands has excellent detail. $425.00.

PLATE 197

PLATE 198

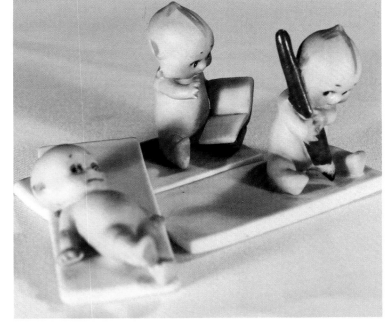

PLATE 199

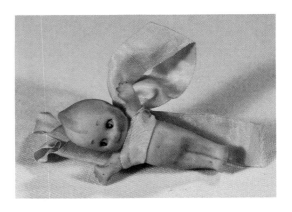

PLATE 200

PLATE 198: 3½" Kewpie "Traveler" with suitcase and umbrella. $400.00.

PLATE 199: 3 different styles of place cards with Kewpie lying down, holding pen, and reading book. The base they are attached to is porcelain. Each - $300.00–500.00.

PLATE 200, 201: 1¾" "Buttonhole" Kewpie with original ribbon. Made in one piece with arms held upward. Backside shows round buttonhole attachment with the Rose O'Neill copyright mark. $165.00.

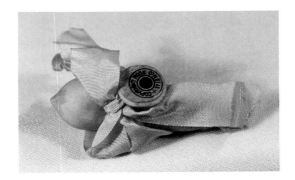

PLATE 201

PLATE 202

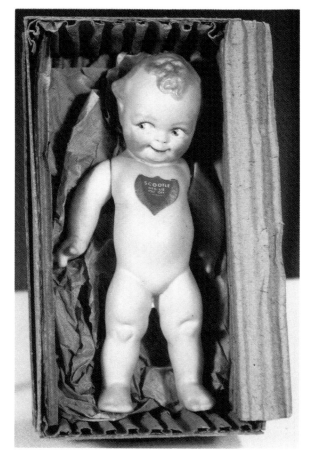

PLATE 203

PLATE 204

PLATE 202: Kewpie with shoulder plate bisque head. Stockinette body, stitched to form feet and hands. Original dress and bonnet. 7" overall. $1,900.00.

PLATE 203: 5½" all bisque "Skootles" that is jointed at shoulders only. Shown with original box. Made in Germany. In box - $1,200.00 up.

PLATE 204: 2" sitting Kewpie holding rose and is attached to original cotton decorated Easter egg. $475.00.

PLATE 205

PLATE 206

PLATE 205: 6" Kewpie in original satin and lace sacque. Jointed at shoulders only. $285.00.

PLATE 206: These Kewpies are both socket heads attached to pincushion bodies. They could have been manufactured this way or hand made. Each - $200.00.

PLATE 207: 1½" sitting Kewpies. One is holding a pen; the other, a mandolin. Each - $185.00–250.00.

PLATE 207

Bathing Dolls

Bathing dolls can be in any position and a great many sizes. They can be lying down, standing, with a base, or without a base. These dolls are made of all bisque and will have painted-on bathing costumes or be nude. They were made in the United States and Germany, but the majority are unmarked so their origins remain unknown. They can be of excellent to very poor quality. Bathing dolls can be priced much higher than "book price" due to position and detail of arms, legs, and amount of workmanship involved in producing the figure. Prices are for dolls with no damage, chips, breaks, hairlines, and must be clean.

EXCELLENT QUALITY OF BISQUE AND ARTIST WORKMANSHIP: 3" - $225.00; 5–6" - $525.00; 8–9" - $800.00 up.

FAIR QUALITY OF BISQUE AND ARTIST WORKMANSHIP: Or marked "Japan." 3" - $85.00; 5–6" - $125.00; 9" - $185.00.

POOR QUALITY: Bisque with high color and poor artist workmanship (crooked eyebrows, lips, etc.) 3" - $35.00; 5–6" - $75.00; 9" - $100.00.

PLATE 208

PLATE 208: 3½" doll with pebbled bathing suit and painted straps. Marked "5684" on leg. Made in Germany. $250.00.

PLATE 209: This 6" bather has very special quality. She has a painted-on face mask and beauty spot. Painted-on hose and shoes. Original wig and clothes. Shown playing modeled mandolin. Made in Germany. $650.00.

PLATE 209

PLATE 210

PLATE 210: 2½" child bathing doll made of all bisque in one piece. She has glass eyes and cut pate with wig. Old catalogs show this tiny doll as part of an Art Deco dresser set with decorative oval mirror tray. The all bisque figure was placed on the mirror to make her own reflection. $200.00.

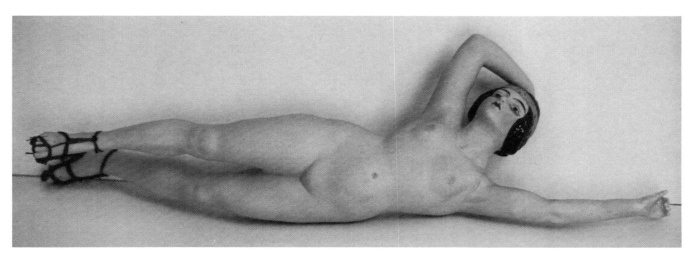

PLATE 211

PLATE 211: Very detailed bathing beauty with much detail to modeling. Has band modeled in hair and all that remains of original costume is her Roman sandals. 6½" - $700.00.

PLATE 212

PLATE 213

PLATE 212: All of these bathing dolls were made in Germany. Some have numbers, such as left center in blue is "5727" and left front in yellow is "6874." In the back row, right in yellow is "4457." Right, center, with gold suit and larger figure, right front, have same number "5684" but different poses. $165.00–485.00.

PLATE 213: These bathing beauties are all made of porcelain except one at far left is made of pewter. The only one that is marked is the far right doll with orange tam and shoes. She is marked "Japan." $165.00–200.00; Pewter - $185.00; Japan - $90.00.

Frozen Charlotte Dolls

Frozen Charlottes and Charlies can be of fine porcelain bisque, stone bisque, china glaze, or part china (such as boots and hair). They can have molded hair, painted bald heads, or take wigs. The majority have no joints with arms and hands extended and legs separated at least to the knees, although some are together. They can be jointed at the shoulders. Generally, they come without clothes, but some may have molded-on clothes. They can also be barefooted or have molded-on shoes or boots.

The tiny Charlottes, up to 3", once were baked into birthday cakes as gifts for children attending parties. The 3–6" dolls were often placed in fine china cups to absorb the instant heat of poured tea so that the cup didn't break. The dolls and the ballad of "Young Charlotte" dates from 1865 and the figures came into being some time after that date. They were very popular by 1880. (See page 92 for the ballad.)

It must be noted that in 1976 a large amount of 15½–16" Charlie figures were produced in Germany and are of excellent quality. It is almost impossible to tell if these reproductions are old or not.

ALL BISQUE: Molded hair, unjointed. 4" - $150.00; 7" - $185.00. Jointed shoulders: 4" - $160.00; 7" - $250.00.

ALL BISQUE, MOLDED-ON CLOTHES OR BONNET: Unjointed. 6" - $450.00; 8" - $550.00. Jointed shoulders: 6" - $175.00; 8" - $285.00.

ALL BISQUE, MOLDED-ON AND PAINTED BOOTS/SHOES: Unjointed. 6" - $200.00; 9" - $385.00. Jointed shoulders: 6" - $285.00; 9" - $485.00.

ALL BISQUE, DRESSED: In original clothes, unjointed. 5" - $135.00; 7" - $185.00. Jointed shoulders: 5" - $175.00; 7" - $285.00.

BLACK CHARLOTTE OR CHARLIE: Unjointed: 3" - $200.00; 5" - $300.00; 7" - $400.00. Jointed shoulders: 3" - $250.00; 5" - $325.00; 7" - $450.00.

STONE BISQUE: Unjointed. 4" - $55.00; 8" - $75.00.

CHINA: Glazed with black or blonde hair, unjointed. 1½" - $55.00; 4–6" - $100.00–165.00; 8–10" - $185.00–250.00; 12" - $325.00.

BALD HEAD, WIG: 5" - $145.00; 7" - $195.00.

CHARLIE: Molded hair, china glaze, flesh color to neck area. 13" - $375.00; 16" - $525.00; 18" - $700.00.

CHARLIE, PORCELAIN: Molded hair, flesh color to neck area. 13" - $425.00; 16" - $625.00; 18" - $825.00.

Young Charlotte

Young Charlotte lived by the mountain side,
    in a wide and lonely spot;
No dwelling there for three miles around,
    except her father's cot.
And yet many a winter's night,
    young swains would gather there,
For her father kept a social board,
    and she was very fair.

Her father liked to see her dressed,
    as fine as a city belle,
For she was the only child he had,
    and he loved his daughter well;
It was New Year's Eve, the sun had set,
    why looks her anxious eye,
So long from the frosty window forth,
    as the merry sleighs pass by.

At the village inn, fifteen miles off
    there's a merry ball tonight;
The piercing air is as cold as death,
    but her heart is warm and light;
But ah! how laughs her beaming eye
    as a well known voice she hears,
And dashing up to the cottage door
    young Charles and sleigh appears.

"O daughter dear" her mother said,
    "this blanket round you fold,
For it is a dreadful night abroad
    and you'll get your death of cold'
"Nay, Mother, nay," Fair Charlotte said,
    and she laughed like a gypsy queen,
"To ride in blankets muffled up I
    can never be seen"

"My silken coat is quite enough,
    It is lined throughout, you know;
Besides I have a silken scarf which
    around my neck I throw."
Her gloves were on, her bonnet tied,
    she jumped into the sleigh
and away they ride up the mountain side
    and o'er the hills away.

There is life in the sounds of the merry bells
    as o'er the hills they go;
What a creaking noise the runner make
    As they bite the frozen snow;
With muffed faces silently,
    o'er five long miles they pass,
When Charles with these frozen words
    the silence broke at last;

"Such a night as this I never saw,
    the reins I scarce can hold."
When Charlotte, shivering faintly said,
    "I am exceedingly cold"
He cracked his whip and urged his team
    more swiftly than before,
Until five other dreary miles in silence
    were passed o'er.

"O see" said Charles, "how fast the
    frost is gathering on my brow."
When Charlotte in a feeble voice said,
    "I am growing warmer now."
And on they ride through the frosty air
    and the glittering cold starlight
Until at last the village inn and ballroom
    are in sight.

They reached the inn and Charles jumped
    out and held his arms to her;
"Why sit you there like a monument without
    the power to stir?"
He called her once, he called her twice,
    she answered not a word;
He called her name again,
    but still she never stirred.

He took her hand in his, O God!
    'twas cold and hard as stone,
He tore the mantle from her brow and
    on her the cold stars shone,
And then into the lighted hall
    her lifeless form he bore,
For Charlotte was a frozen corpse and
    words spoke nevermore.

He sat himself down by her side and
    the bitter tears did flow,
And he said "My young intended bride,
    I never more shall know."
He threw his arms around her neck
    and kissed her marble brow,
And his thoughts went back to where she said,
    "I'm growing warmer now."

He bore her out into the sleigh
    and with her he drove home,
And when he reached the cottage door,
    O how her parents mourned;
They mourned the loss of their daughter dear
    while Charles mourned o'er their gloom,
Until with grief his heart did break,
    and they slumber in one tomb.

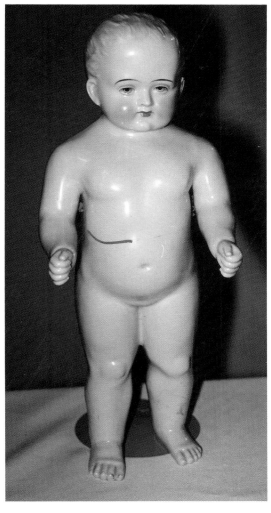

PLATE 214

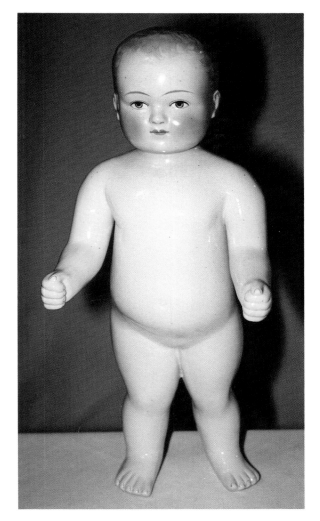

PLATE 215

PLATE 214: Beautiful 15" "Frozen Charlie" with deeply modeled hair and a full pink luster under glaze. Full cheeks, molded eyelids, and detailed fingers and toes. Made in Germany. $700.00.

PLATE 215: 15" blonde "Frozen Charlie" with pink luster on head and upper neck. Has detailed nails on hands and feet. Made in Germany. $600.00.

PLATE 216: 3½" bisque "Frozen Charlie" with molded hair and painted features. Good details to hands and feet. Made in Germany. $150.00.

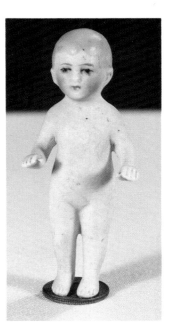

PLATE 216

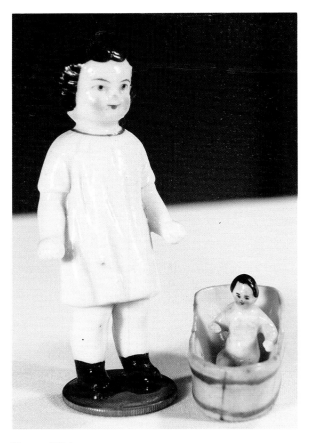

PLATE 217

PLATE 218

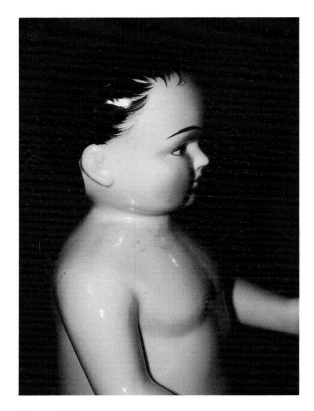

PLATE 219

PLATE 217: 5" early "Frozen Charlotte" made of very lightweight porcelain. Excellent hairdo with partly exposed ears. Bare feet. Made in Germany. $175.00.

PLATE 218: 3" glazed china "Frozen Charlotte" with painted-on boots and neckline. The 1" sitting "Charlotte" in tub is also glazed china. The attached tub is made of porcelain but glazed inside. Made in Germany. 3" - $95.00; 1" in tub - $60.00.

PLATE 219: This side view of a 15" "Frozen Charlie" shows the brush marks around the face. He has brown painted eyes and a light pink luster down the neck. Made in Germany. $700.00.

PLATE 220

PLATE 221

PLATE 220: On the left is a 5" "Frozen Charlotte" with pink skin tones and a very unusual hairdo. Shown with a 4½" "Frozen Charlotte" with "low brow" hairdo and has unpainted molded-on boots. 5" - $185.00; 4½" - $175.00.

PLATE 221: 2" blonde and black hair "Frozen Charlottes." The one with black hair has a "civil war/covered wagon" hairdo and is very chubby. Each - $55.00.

PLATE 222: 4½" "Frozen Charlie" that has eggshell thin bisque. Side part hairdo and spread legs. Flesh color bisque. $200.00.

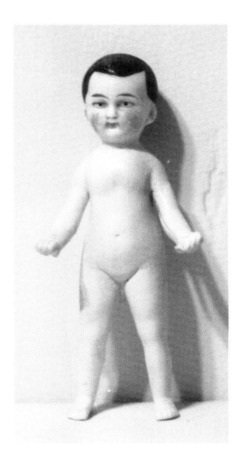

PLATE 222

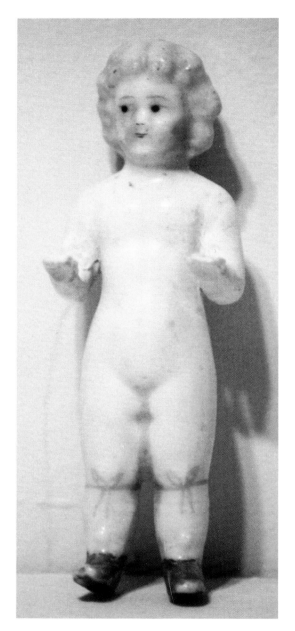

PLATE 223

PLATE 224

PLATE 223: 3" "Frozen Charlotte" with full blonde hairdo and side glancing painted eyes. She wears gold luster painted-on boots with pink ties. $150.00.

PLATE 224: 2" "Frozen Charlotte" with blonde hairdo and modeled tiara. (To find anything modeled into the hairdo is unusual.) Has blue painted-on boots. $150.00.

PLATE 225: 4½" and 2½" black "Frozen Charlottes." Both have "flat top" hairdos. The taller version has arms molded to body down to wrists. 4½" - $140.00; 2½" - $95.00.

PLATE 225

PLATE 226: 2" and 5" "Frozen Charlottes." The 2" doll has arms raised higher than most and a "flat top" hairdo. The 5" doll has excellent face color and sausage curls around head. 2" - $60.00; 5" - $165.00.

PLATE 226

PLATE 227: A doll room or shadow box style display are perfect for displaying "Frozen Charlotte and Charlie" dolls. Most of these dolls will not adapt to a doll stand.

PLATE 227

Piano Babies

Piano babies were just that – figurines, usually in pairs, used on top of a piano along with a Victorian piano scarf. They came in several sizes with some being quite large. The quality of workmanship ranges from the finest artistry to the five-and-dime store variety.

Most were made in Germany from the 1880's to the 1930's. They were produced by the finest porcelain factories of that era, such as Gebruder Heubach, Kestner, Limbach, and Dressel, Kister and Company.

Piano babies are really unjointed figurines, but are acceptable into any doll collection. They have molded hair, painted features, molded-on clothes, and come in a variety of positions.

> **EXCELLENT QUALITY:** Extremely fine artist workmanship with backs of figures painted. They will have applied or modeled bows, items in their hands, curled toes, intaglio eyes, and deeply modeled hair. The overall piece is in excellent condition. 4" - $190.00; 8" - $450.00; 12" - $750.00 up; 16" - $900.00 up.

> **MEDIUM QUALITY:** May not be painted on back side of figure. 4" - $125.00; 8" - $265.00; 12" - $400.00; 16" - $550.00.

> **HOLDING ANIMAL, IN CHAIR, WITH FLOWERS, OR WITH OTHER LARGE OBJECTS:** Excellent quality: 4" - $250.00; 8" - $450.00; 12" - $825.00; 16" - $1,200.00 up. Medium quality: 4" - $165.00; 8" - $250.00; 12" - $400.00; 16" - $800.00.

PLATE 228: 3½" piano baby with dove on its shoulder. Made in Germany and marked "968.3." Excellent details. $250.00.

PLATE 228

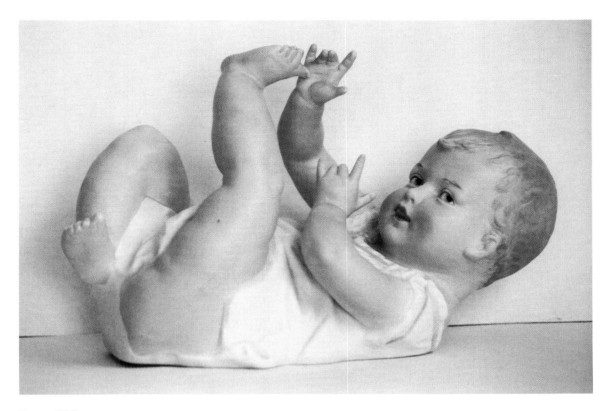

PLATE 229

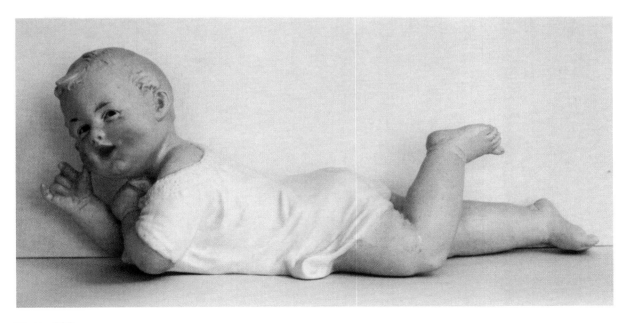

PLATE 230

PLATE 229: Beautiful German-made piano baby with intaglio eyes and modeled-on clothes. Excellent detail to modeling. 12" - $750.00 up.

PLATE 230: 7" long piano baby that lays on its stomach. It has intaglio eyes and wide open/closed mouth. Made in Germany. $425.00.

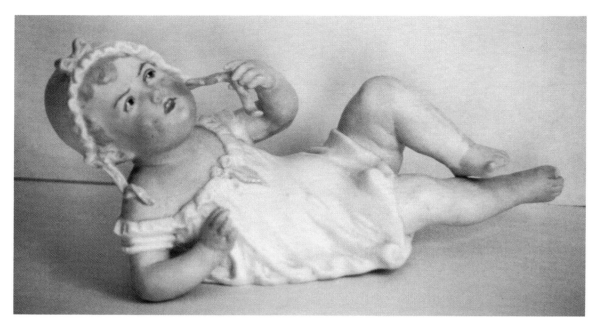

PLATE 231

PLATE 231: Piano baby with good quality modeling detail, intaglio eyes, and molded-on bonnet. 8" - $300.00.

PLATE 232: 8" and 3" piano babies that are modeled alike. Excellent detail to hands and feet, which are modeled separately. Both have open/closed mouths. The larger one has more detailed hair and features. 3" - $180.00; 8" - $460.00.

PLATE 232

PLATE 233

PLATE 234

PLATE 233: **Pair of 8" German piano babies marked "2185." Excellent detail and intaglio eyes. Each -
$450.00.**

PLATE 234: **7" piano babies with both made in one piece. Deeply modeled hair, painted features, and both
are of excellent quality. The one on the left is marked "Germany/4001/ ◇ L.B." The figure on the right
was made by Gebruder Heubach. Both were made in Germany. Each - $375.00.**

PLATE 235

PLATE 236

PLATE 235: Beautiful Gebruder Heubach figure holding rabbit's ear. Egg is vase and stands 8" overall. Excellent detail to entire piece. $950.00.
PLATE 236: 4" piano baby with excellent detail to its features. Has porcelain fired netting trim and one arm away from figure. $250.00.

Other Doll Books By
America's Leading Doll Author
PATRICIA SMITH

Antique Collector's Dolls, Volumes I & II, each $17.95

Collector's Encyclopedia of
    Madame Alexander Dolls...$24.95

French Dolls in Color, 3rd Series $14.95

Madame Alexander Dolls..$19.95

Madame Alexander Dolls Price Guide #17 ....$9.95

Modern Collector's Dolls Volumes I–V, each..................................$17.95

Patricia Smith's Doll Values,
    Antique To Modern, Eighth Series..$12.95

Shirley Temple Dolls, Volumes I & II, each...................................$17.95

World of Alexander-kins $19.95

Order from your favorite dealer or
COLLECTOR BOOKS

P.O. Box 3009
Paducah, KY 42002–3009

When ordering by mail, please add $2.00 postage and handling for the first book,
30¢ for each additional book.

Schroeder's Antiques Price Guide

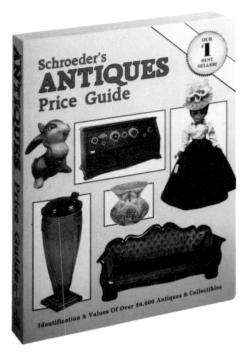

Schroeder's Antiques Price Guide has become THE household name in the antiques & collectibles field. Our team of editors works year-round with more than 200 contributors to bring you our #1 best-selling book on antiques & collectibles.

With more than 50,000 items identified & priced, Schroeder's is a must for the collector & dealer alike. If it merits the interest of today's collector, you'll find it in Schroeder's. Each subject is represented with histories and background information. In addition, hundreds of sharp original photos are used each year to illustrate not only the rare and unusual, but the everyday "fun-type" collectibles as well — not postage stamp pictures, but large close-up shots that show important details clearly.

Our editors compile a new book each year. Never do we merely change prices. Accuracy is our primary aim. Prices are gathered over the entire year previous to publication, from ads and personal contacts. Then each category is thoroughly checked to spot inconsistencies, listings that may not be entirely reflective of actual market dealings, and lines too vague to be of merit. Only the best of the lot remains for publication. You'll find Schroeder's Antiques Price Guide the one to buy for factual information and quality.

No dealer, collector or investor can afford not to own this book. It is available from your favorite bookseller or antiques dealer at the low price of $12.95. If you are unable to find this price guide in your area, it's available from Collector Books, P.O. Box 3009, Paducah, KY 42002-3009 at $12.95 plus $2.00 for postage and handling.

8½ x 11", 608 Pages   **$12.95**

COLLECTOR BOOKS
A Division of Schroeder Publishing Co., Inc.